I Know the Rules!

I SHARE!

By Bray Jacobson

Gareth Stevens Publishing

Please visit our website, www.garethstevens.com. For a free color catalog of all our high-quality books, call toll free 1-800-542-2595 or fax 1-877-542-2596.

Library of Congress Cataloging-in-Publication Data
Names: Jacobson, Bray, author.
Title: I share! / Bray Jacobson.
Description: Buffalo, New York : Gareth Stevens Publishing, [2024] | Series: I know the rules! | Includes index.
Identifiers: LCCN 2022051552 (print) | LCCN 2022051553 (ebook) | ISBN 9781538286685 (library binding) | ISBN 9781538286678 (paperback) | ISBN 9781538286692 (ebook)
Subjects: LCSH: Sharing–Juvenile literature. | Benevolence–Juvenile literature.
Classification: LCC BJ1533.G4 J348 2024 (print) | LCC BJ1533.G4 (ebook) | DDC 177/.7–dc23/eng/20221230
LC record available at https://lccn.loc.gov/2022051552
LC ebook record available at https://lccn.loc.gov/2022051553

Published in 2024 by
Gareth Stevens Publishing
2544 Clinton Street
Buffalo, NY 14224

Designer: Claire Wrazin
Editor: Kristen Nelson

Photo credits: cover EvgeniiAnd/Shutterstock.com; p. 5 Twinsterphoto/Shutterstock.com; pp. 7, 24 (crayons) Daniel Jedzura/Shutterstock.com; p. 9 Alexander Safonov/Shutterstock.com; p. 11 GagliardiPhotography/Shutterstock.com; pp. 13, 24 (snack) littlenySTOCK/Shutterstock.com; p. 15 Iryna Inshyna/Shutterstock.com; p. 17 Tomsickova Tatyana/Shutterstock.com; pp. 19, 24 (apple) Hananeko_Studio/Shutterstock.com; p. 21 Billion Photos/Shutterstock.com; p. 23 Natalia Lebedinskaia/Shutterstock.com.

Printed in the United States of America

CPSIA compliance information: Batch #CSGS24: For further information contact Gareth Stevens, at 1-800-542-2595.

Contents

I share!
It is a rule at school.

Dennis is drawing
a picture.
He has a box
of crayons.

HAPPY FATHER'S DAY!

Patti asks to use
the crayons.
She says please.
Dennis shares!

Leighton has
the big ball.
She passes it to Don.
They are sharing.

There is one snack left.
Drew wants it.
Holden wants it.

The teacher cuts it
in half.
The boys share
the snack.

I share at home.
I let my brother play
with my car.
He gives it back!

Andrea's apple
tastes good.
She gives her mom
a piece.

They share the fruit!

How can you share?

Words to Know

apple

crayon

snack

Index